CREATING

MANIFESTATION

POWER

Into The Now

Harness your Inner Power, Create
Abundance in your Life

WRITTEN BY

EVA GAJIC

BALBOA.PRESS
A DIVISION OF HAY HOUSE

Balboa Press books may be ordered through booksellers or by contacting:

Balboa Press
A Division of Hay House
1663 Liberty Drive
Bloomington, IN 47403
www.balboapress.com.au
AU TFN: 1 800 844 925 (Toll Free inside Australia)
AU Local: (02) 8310 7086 (+61 2 8310 7086 from outside Australia)

Print information available on the last page.

ISBN: 979-8-7652-0010-0 (sc)
ISBN: 979-8-7652-0011-7 (hc)
ISBN: 979-8-7652-0009-4 (e)

Library of Congress Control Number: 2024914520

Balboa Press rev. date: 09/16/2024

THE POWER LIES DEEP WITHIN

Acknowledgements

This book is dedicated to my beautiful
parents with whom I lovely dearly
and hold close to my heart
To my late father and mother,
Josip Ivan Gajic & Nada Gajic

Contents

What you think you become.
What you feel you attract.
What you imagine you create.

- Buddha

Preface

Dear Creators, let me take you on a journey of remembrance. A remembering of your innate divine qualities. Throughout this book, I reveal the truth about our reality, expressed through my connection to higher consciousness. I share these words of wisdom to enrich the reader with many truths that we all understand were once known but have been lost in translation—forgotten. It is my hope that my words will ignite a remembering from within that will motivate you to Create at Will and Desire your reality the way you want to live it. After all, we are all creative beings, and you are a Creator! Before we commence, I advise you keep an Open Mind and with an Open Heart - Let the Journey begin ...

Introduction

A Holographic Universe—Your Reality

What if I were to tell you a story but the story is not fantasy but a story of our current reality, more real than our physical existence, more diverse and unlimited than we have all been taught to be believe or you can imagine or comprehend in a finite mind. Would you not want to create at will and be what you want to be at any time? I do not know anyone who would deliberately create a life they were not happy to live, but many are living this way, not awakened to the fact that we have inherent abilities within each and every one of us.

We are Masters of our reality.

Throughout time, until today, humanity has searched for our origins, searching for truths to our existence. There is this constant search to seek and find answers to everything in life.

Our quest to seek answers far and wide has never stopped; today, in our current reality, we are still searching. Our search continues and has led humankind out into the universe, star systems, and galaxies. Our constant search comes from a deep yearning from within each of us to understand what this life is all about and to prove to ourselves we are not alone and that there are other worlds and civilisations. There are other worlds out there much like our own.

We as humans are always seeking a great technology capable of linking our civilisation with others. In our search we have come across the greatest minds in history, from Hermes Trismegistus and Aristotle to Einstein, Nikola Tesla, and Wernher von Braun. We've built the Giza pyramids with exact precision and in alignment with the stars; developed rockets capable of travelling to the moon; with humanity taking its steps across its surface, as well as *Voyager* and *Cassini* and other sophisticated robotic spacecraft designed to travel and investigate planets in our vicinity and beyond ... so much to uncover.

There is, however, only so much knowledge that can be presented to humanity as this point in time; this is as far as it goes for now. What if I were to let you in on a secret that has been around for eons if not from the beginning of time? This secret is only a reminder to you ... that *you* are the greatest technology.

Your power lies deep within you and cannot be found in the outside world. Would you even believe it? You probably wouldn't but the reality is—You are it!

The great technology humanity has been speaking about for thousands of years is inside each and every single one of us: we are the technology. We have a physicality that is constantly replenishing itself; our cells are always being restored, and furthermore we are made up of energy that is constantly flowing through us and in us. As we all know, energy can neither be created nor destroyed. Scientists and quantum physicists believe that almost all of our body mass comes from the kinetic energy of elementary particles such as quarks and gluons. It is noted that elementary particles such as quarks are the ultimate building blocks of the visible matter in the universe and reside deep within the atoms that make up our bodies and even within the protons and neutrons that make up our atomic nuclei. The protons, neutrons, and electrons are the subatomic particles that make up the atomic particles that form our body.

Whilst most of the cells in our body regenerate, the particles that make up those cells have existed for millions of millennia. We have elements in us that also exist in burning and exploding stars.[1]

Everything that we are searching for in the universe and how it works and this constant search for answers can be found by going within. This is how truly marvellous we all are.

> "You have elements within you that form the beautiful stars shining brightly at night. You are a shining Star."

---

[1] The Universe, Quarks What are they? By Keith Cooper Nov 201, 2022

If you look at the very makeup of the human body, you will see that the cells of our body are made up of atomic particles banded together with energy gyrating around subatomic particles. In fact, we have trillions of atoms in one cell, and in our body we have trillions of cells. The average human at rest produces 100 watts of power. Now that is truly amazing, is it not?

In our essence we are energetic beings. We have the ability to control situations that come to us by manipulating the energy around us. We in effect are here to become master manipulators of energy.

The words we speak, the thoughts we think, our mindset is all energy. We have the innate ability to control this energy as "master manipulators of energy". We control the dial through Vibration and frequency, and just as a tuning fork, we magnetise all events that come to us, good or bad.

The truth to our existence and our reality can diminish our sense of logic and reasoning. We are not taught that we are energy, we are not shown how truly marvellous we are at an atomic level. We are not shown that we magnetise energy or shown that we control our surroundings and environment.

Human logic and reasoning are a conditioned state. Humans are creatures of habit. We really do have a limited understanding of our current reality and it was designed this way. Our reality is a multidimensional reality, but we are not taught this or shown how this is possible. We have only been shown a reality where life is happening to us, and it is deliberately presented this way.

We all live in multidimensional reality. This multidimensional existence means that all our experiences exist simultaneously, and the ability to tap into any experience we choose is very real and achievable. Tapping into any experience is how we can manipulate energy and bring like events vibrating at our frequency to us.

The universe we live in today is made up of events all occurring at the same time as the one we are in now. It will sound strange if this is all new to you, but all situations past, present, and future are occurring in the present moment.

This present moment is now.

In our physical reality we perceive events in a linear progression, where everything has a beginning and an ending, there is a stop and a start. When people are told that they create their reality, a lot of them find it hard to accept. The truth is that most of humanity go about their daily lives on autopilot their entire lives, not realising that we have the inherent ability to change or control events yet to unfold in the future. The dynamic changes when we understand that we *can* change events that unfold in the future and furthermore we *can* modify our past situations.

Our world is multidimensional.

In time we will all understand and grasp that we are powerful and infinite in nature. By this I am referring to who we are, what we are.

"*Who am I?*"

We are all individual emanations of source energy, much like rays of light coming from a sun. We all have expanded from one single point of consciousness out in all directions. We are an expression of Source energy; some may call it higher consciousness, and some call it God. It all refers to the same thing. I like to call it Source energy, higher consciousness, or All that is. Whatever feels right for you.

Each one of us is an individual expression of consciousness experiencing our life journey here on Earth, to feel, touch, and create.

You are here to Create at Will.

These words you are reading are highlighting what you already know at a soul level. Throughout all existence all beings, not just here on earth but throughout entire star systems and galaxies, are seeking to understand themselves –looking for answers to their existence, looking for their purpose, searching for more of everything, constantly seeking knowledge, constantly creating.

The search to be whole again comes from a memory that there is more to our existence here on Earth. It goes much deeper.

We all have an innate knowingness of who we are, and we all know we are a part of something much bigger and that everything we encompass in life is in divine order.

*We are a part of Consciousness that is
whole and pure.*

There are no mistakes in this universe; everything we do and all decisions we take in life come from a choice that we make. Rest assured you won't be judged for the decisions you make in life, as it is the growth and expansion of yourself that is forever evolving. As we are all uniquely different from one another, we all grow and evolve at different rates and speeds. This is why you are the only one accountable for the actions you take and also the one to be honoured for the achievements you make.

Furthermore, we are more than human. We are divine beings inside a physical body, with the ability to create our reality whichever way we choose. What a marvellous technology we all are.

Right now, the world we live in is a world where not everyone is ready to expand their consciousness, and this is okay. As we all are individual expressions of consciousness, we are all unique, and we all expand and resonate differently.

All soul journeys have different paths. Some take longer to awaken and become aware, whilst a large number are ready now.

Humans are creatures of habit and routine. Just as it takes us years or more to develop our adult personalities, we're also developing behaviours and habits that will stay with us for a lifetime. Unfortunately, some of those behaviours and habits are not always healthy or helpful to us.

We need to shed old beliefs, and this does takes time. After all, you have carried them your entire life, and in most cases, belief systems are carried through from generation to generation. If a belief you carry doesn't feel right to you, then you must ask why. You are in charge of the vessel—the body you walk around in. Nurture your physicality and mind with a healthy attitude and mindset. Surround yourself with everything you love and what brings you joy.

You are the only one responsible for your life; no one else is to be blamed for the burdens or misfortunes you carry. This is the hardest lesson to learn, for many are not yet ready to accept accountability. We as humans have long walked around with blindfolds on, and now the veil has been lifted. Every action we take is a *choice*. There are no mistakes in the universe. All is in divine order. After all, you choose to focus on a certain thing over another.

You choose to allow memories to fill you with sadness, hate, fear and regret. A scenario playing over and over in your mind that doesn't eventuate.

Everything is a *choice*, and the choice is up to you and what you decide to put your attention to.

You are very powerful; your words are powerful; your thoughts are powerful.

Energy can only flow where your attention goes. Therefore, set your attention upon something beautiful. Truly try it. Everything in our existence flows, and so must you. You are no different. No matter how hard or difficult things may be, you need to push through and flow, as resistance won't allow new growth, and you cannot move on to greener pastures if you block the natural order of life that requires everything to flow. You *must* flow with everything in life. I guarantee you, no matter what situation you are facing, I will impart these words on to you: "*and this too shall pass.*" It is the only natural order. Take comfort in these words, for this is the only way.

These words typed on this page in this book reveal many truths and take you to forgotten memories that lie dormant within. I may even zone into areas you wouldn't imagine, and I do this as I am helping you understand the power you have, so you can be the best version of yourself and live the life you choose. I will provide examples and methods that will guide and show you how to tap into your own Manifestation Power. Wake up the dormant self that sleeps within and learn to trust that inner voice that resides deep within.

There are many books on manifestation that tell the tale that if we just wish for things to be a certain way, they will automatically appear. However, there is an art to Manifestation, and it does take time and effort.

If you have found yourself reading these words, this is no coincidence, and if you have heard this sentence before, it is time to act now and create the reality you deserve.

What does this all mean?

You no longer need to live a life that is giving you no joy, no need to live in fear, or live in a reality that is happening to you. There is an abundance out there for all who desire to seek it and there is more than enough for everyone.

As the old parable says:

> *"Keep knocking, and it will be opened to you.*
> *For everyone who asks - receives.*
> *He/she who seeks - finds.*
> *To him/her who knocks it will be opened."*

If you have the motivation and the desire, then with an open mind you have the potential to Create Manifestation Power.

Eva Gajic

VOLUME ONE

An introduction to Consciousness

ONE

The Mind

The All is Mind—The Universe is Mental.
-Hermetic Philosophy

Everything in the universe is created through our minds. All is mind. All that we see around us—our environment, the people, the circumstances—is of our own doing. It is well known that "the Mind is Just like a muscle—the more we exercise it, the stronger it becomes and the more it expands."[2] If we look even deeper, our minds are more powerful than many are aware.

---

[2] Idowu Koyenikan, *Wealth for All: Living a Life of Success at the Edge of Your Ability.*

To understand the mind, you need to understand who you are at an atomic level. First, to state the obvious, we are human beings living on planet Earth. Our physical bodies are the vessels in which our true nature resides, our spirits/souls. We are made up of energy that is vibrating and gyrating constantly. We have organs within our bodies made up of molecules, molecules made up of trillions of cells, cells made of trillions of atoms, atoms made up of trillions of subatomic particles, and at the very core, we have energy. Our physical body, like all matter, vibrates at a certain speed of ten hertz in order to appear solid. Our light body, the soul, needs our physical body to anchor us into this reality, given that our current reality is physical and dense. Without our physical bodies, we could not move around and be a part of this world.

We Are Here to Experience

This existence of ours on Earth is a touchy-feely experience. We need to feel and touch everything. As our bodies grow older and our souls within evolve further, the need to touch and feel everything lessens to a degree. You may have heard the saying "I've been there, done that," or you may talk to an older person who will confidently say, "There is nothing more left for me to do." Would it not be wonderful if this touchy-feely experience of your life is the experience you have given to yourself rather than one that is happening to you?

Why So Much Emphasis on the Mind?
Why Is It So Important?

The mind is consciousness, and consciousness is everywhere and in everything. Consciousness is enriched with the knowledge of all that is and ever will be. When we begin to understand and become aware we are consciousness, this source of knowledge can be accessed. If you can understand this concept—that all is mind, and mind is consciousness—it can change you at a cellular level. This is self-awareness.

There are a lot of topics on the mind. People often view the mind as connected to the brain and tap their foreheads as an indication that this is the only place the mind can reside—in the brain. However, it is not this way. The mind is not just located in the brain, as some believe; it encompasses our whole being, our entire body. It is our consciousness, and consciousness is everything. Everything in all existence is one consciousness or, in other terms, one living mind.

According to science, the difference between our brains and our minds is that "the Brain is physical and is the centre of our nervous system, which coordinates the movements, thoughts, and feelings. The mind however is mental and refers to a person's understanding and his/her conscience and refers to a person's thought process."[3]

---

[3] S, P. (2011, January 8). *Difference Between Mind and Brain.* Difference Between Similar Terms and Objects. http://www.differencebetween.net/ science/health/difference-between-mind-and-brain/.

Throughout time, all civilisations that existed before us understood that the mind is powerful. They knew that what we think about, we truly do bring about. Even more, the words we speak have a power to them, just like our thoughts. Our thoughts must appear in our minds before we verbalise our intentions.

We are made up of energy. We are master manipulators of this energy, and we control it through the very words we speak and what comes to us. It is the same when you are thinking about something: you generate an electrical charge around these thoughts like a transmission tower that then sends signals of your thoughts out into the universe. Then everything that is in tune with your thoughts is drawn back to you.
For example, I may think about a friend I have not seen for ages. A few weeks later, this person may call me, or I may run into this person. I was just thinking about this person before they called or showed up, and my thought of this person drew them to me like a magnet, good or bad.

When we think about every single action we have taken in our lives—every second of them—we have first visualised the action in the mind's eye before carrying it out. Furthermore, when we visualise situations or events, we also develop a corresponding emotion.

The ability to harness control over our thoughts is vital. Our thoughts bring to us our circumstances, good or bad. Therefore, we must control what thoughts enter our minds and monitor the corresponding emotion we feel when we think a certain thought. At all times, how we feel when we receive a thought is a good indicator of whether we are thinking bad or good thoughts. For example, a bad thought will make you feel bad, and a good thought will make you feel good.

When we become aware of our thoughts, we start developing a state of awareness in the present moment and begin aligning with source energy. Currently, in our society, many tend to fall out of alignment with themselves too often. Many people are constantly thinking too far ahead, and it can become detrimental to their physical health. Illnesses appear, and in most cases, the scenes we play out in our minds never actually occur, and all the stress and self-talk served no purpose but to cause fear and prevent a natural flow of energy. For example, when we look at traffic ahead of us, we assume we are never going to get out of it.

Eventually we do. At most, there was no queue. We looked too far ahead and thought the impossible. But we always make it. Life is the same. Look too far ahead, and you will fall out of alignment with yourself.

We all know that person who in every conversation will focus on the negative aspects of something or see the problem with everything. It can be exhausting, and they will feel validated when errors do pop up. The reality is they drew it to themselves. But thinking this way will only make you sick. Try something different. When something new is presented to you, rather than criticise everything, be open-minded and think brighter, more uplifting thoughts. If you stay in the present, you will always make it. It is very important to understand that we can only ever control the moment we have now, for this moment is all you truly ever have.

All Creation Occurs in the Now

5

The now is formed out of a reality that is constantly shifting. There is no constant in our existence apart from the one consciousness we are a part of. When you start on this path to unravelling your creative power of manifestation, you can only do so by viewing your goals as already being achieved, living in the end result. You need not just believe in *that something* to achieve success, for that is mere admiration.

You must become that which you seek in your life. If you desire more love in your life, you do not go about telling everyone that you believe in love and then expect it to come your way. No, you must become love. Give love, express love, *be* love. If you seek money, the same applies. You do not believe that one day you will achieve it; you need to become it by adopting a wealthy and successful mindset. Feel, see, and smell abundance all around you. *Be* abundance. That which you seek will pervade your whole consciousness if you allow it. When you do, you are in the process of being what you are here to do—to create at will your reality.

In My Dreams, There Are No Limits

Shaping your reality the way you seek requires work. Unfortunately, when we are in our adolescent years, we are taught to do things a certain way. It starts from the old adage "You must work hard to be successful." This is a limited sentence. It also isn't enticing at all; it gives the impression that to be successful, you must go through tough and hard times to meet success. I am certain that once the success dies down, tough and hard times will be there to greet you again in one shape or another. Why? Life must be hard to have great things; this is why. This is what you believe, and therefore it can only be given.

The universe only understands the word *yes*, and if this is what you are thinking, then this is what you shall receive. Working hard is not a motto to live by. Our mindsets need to shift, and we need to rewire the brain in effect to replace outdated, unhealthy habits with those that are in alignment with a mindset that is unlimited and will allow us to reach our full potential.

A shift needs to occur, and beliefs must be altered. What we say to ourselves daily or think in our minds really matters. Changing a simple sentence from "Working really hard" to "I always achieve successful outcomes in all areas in my life," you will notice that the whole dynamic shifts from a limited reality to one that is unlimited, abundant, and successful. Magnetically, this can only draw to you everything in existence that is vibrating success. You will find the ones who say, "You have to work hard to get somewhere in life." They had these words relayed to them, and this sentiment became a belief formed at early stages of their formative years.

Mastering your reality really does depend on your ability to manifest at will a reality that is of your choosing, to tap into the emotion, and to become that which you desire.

The journey of mastery relies heavily on your thoughts and what you are thinking. If you notice that your thoughts are primarily negative, then this must change, it cannot be any other way. I am not saying for you to wish for a new house. Wishing for things is simply just that—wishing, nothing more. True change must take place, and it must occur at a deeper level—an energetic one.

If you find that your thoughts are primarily negative, then find the strength within, and take control of your life. You need to shift your focus onto happy events, happy situations, and engage in positive self-talk.

The first rule of manifestation is on the basis that positive affirmations are used in place of negative ones. The second rule is embedding the thought through repetition of the affirmation. Refer to the example below.

Example One:

If you are finding yourself in challenging circumstance, you must change the words you use to describe yourself or others and your situation and how you pitch yourself to others.

Instead of saying this:

"I always have bad things happen to me."

or

"Nothing good ever happens to me."

You must end this now and replace it with affirmations such as

"I am successful in everything I set out to achieve."

and

"Good things always happen to me on a continuous basis."

You would in this instance take the new affirmation and repeat it several times a day; make it your mantra. When you get up in the morning, say it ten times over and before you go to bed at night.

You need to seed the new thought, embed it into your subconscious, and allow it to replace the old negative thought patterns until it has materialised into your current reality. If this is done properly, with will and Desire, you can achieve your new desired state. Getting your head around this will take time and effort, and initially you will find it very hard. This is quite normal as you are rewiring your brain for greatness, and this will take time. You will also observe the situation you are in, which may look bleak, and affirm you are successful. This may feel like a lie. Or it may appear nothing is happening, tempting you to give up trying.

It will take time, and it will require you to make the effort each day. If you are serious about changing your life, you will have the drive, the passion, the motivation, and the Desire to do the work required to transform your life.

You are an artist, and your life is the composition. You pick your theme, the colours, the people and events; every single detail is created by you. This is why Manifestation is an art. You need to be able to transmute your words and make them work for you.

Your intentions are to be embedded into your subconscious mind, and you do this by using affirmations, just like the ones outlined in the earlier example. You can create them any way you desire, provided they are statements believable to you, as you do have to become that which you seek, and you need to seed the intention.

What is seeding?

Seeding an intention is much like planting a seed into the soil and watering it daily. At first you won't see anything for some time, but with consistency and repeated watering, the seed will sprout and grow. If you stop watering the seed, nothing can come from it.

The intentions require the same attention, dedication, and willingness to repeat your mantra until it has formed into your reality. In most cases, all so subtly it will appear.

The universe always provides. There is a magnetic link like a giant interconnected web that connects you to everything in existence. Every day the human brain processes thousands and thousands of thoughts. Therefore, it matters where you place your focus and what you focus on regularly. Just like the magnetic link, you draw to yourself exactly what you are thinking about every second of the day.

The key is being able to manipulate your energy so you are able to draw to you your desired outcome. If you are thinking and speaking negatively about yourself or others, whether aloud or silently, either way you will draw to you like a magnet exactly those situations that you dread so much. The Universe does not understand the difference between good or bad; it just understands that it will deliver to you what you are thinking about regularly.

*The Universe will always give back to you what
you send out.*

This is a hard truth, but a truth it is, and it is very real and an important lesson. Many call this Karma, but the term has been misunderstood for a very long time. Many use the term *Karma* for all things bad. It is not this way.

All things, good or bad, will return to you if this is what you are sending out. Our human body is a receiver of information, and we also send signals out at the same time. Therefore, if your signal is set to negativity, you will receive it; however, if your signal is set to positive, this will instead come to you.

The sea of consciousness that we are part is made up of frequency and vibrations, and our bodies may as well be a transmission tower. We have the power to change the transmission. We control the dial; change the settings so as to draw good things to you.

There is an alchemical process that takes place when we think thoughts, and we have the inherent ability to transmute any thought that enters our mind from one state to another. The sages all knew and understood this. In fact, the Oxford dictionary defines *transmutation* as "an act of changing, or of being changed, into something different".

Transmute the thoughts that enter your mind. Clear negative thoughts from the mind. Make it a clear slate. It can be difficult for someone to make proper decisions and find on-time solutions if their mind is not yet clear from negativity.

TWO

The Power of Mindfulness

Listen to the Silence; it has much to Say.
-Anonymous-

Silence.
Close your eyes ...
Focus on your breath and just *be* ...
Allow your body to withdraw from the outside noise, and observe in silence, with no expectation, the real you. The side of you that is not the body but is far greater.
Life events doesn't happen to someone. They must be given permission to allow them to occur to a person, good or bad. You are the only person responsible for your life.

"'In this silence I am one with myself."

The biggest dilemma in this world today, which no one is talking about, is that "*You control your destiny.*" Imagine if everyone in the whole world becomes conscious of their thoughts and understands they can at will change their circumstances just with a simple shift in perception.

The very fabric of our existence will be a completely different one. Our planet will be vibrating at an elevated level, a level that will see humanity enter a new era of existence—one of Peace, Oneness, Kindness, and balance. There will be more than enough for everyone. No war, no poverty, no illnesses.

How wonderful this sounds. But it is true and attainable. Understand that we are evolving towards greatness. This book I am writing is one of many out there teaching humanity to join this evolutionary shift towards a new Earth.

The shift has already commenced; look around you. Planet Earth has woken up. We see the floods, the earthquakes. Mother Earth is letting humanity know we are shifting into a new era—an era when all humans will remember who they all are. Remember this: We are for this world, not of this world. Also understand Planet Earth is a being that is conscious. When humanity vibrates with high vibrations, we help Earth evolve.

> "*There are no constants in this existence, only one sea of consciousness of All that is.*"

The Remembering

We are brought into this world forgetting every
life we have lived with the deliberate intention to
remember who we are—who you are.
You would have a hard to time expanding and
growing consciously if you remembered
everything. You would not want to incarnate on
Earth.

"WHO ARE YOU ...?"

You are a spirit inside a human body having an
earthly experience in schoolroom Earth.
Your lives are the lessons you must pass.
The key to passing this exam is learning to
go within. Therefore, it is with great joy that I
share this with you and remind you of your
innate qualities.
To be mindful and aware is so very important that
it will help you find your way back home. Not the
temporary one you have while you are incarnated
on Earth, but your true home.
When a person becomes attuned to themselves
and their surroundings, there is a peace and
serenity, an alignment with source energy.
This is Mindfulness.

Mindfulness requires discipline. You must have
the Motivation, Will, and Desire. It is the only way
to tap into the Infinite, Universal supply of All
that is to achieve your goals and live your
dreams.

A disciplined mind is a mindful one, and Mindfulness is a form of Self-Reflection. It allows you to really look at your life and get in touch with your higher consciousness with Source.

When faced with the big-picture questions of life —when you really ask yourself, *What do I want?* *What do I need?*—you will find that what you think you need is not what you truly need.

At most when people learn they are in control of creating their life, it is easy to wish for something their higher self knows isn't for them. In this moment in time, it may be a new car or winning the lottery; it could even be a new home.

> *"Everything in existence is a choice;*
> *Everything is in divine order.*
> *There are no mistakes."*

You will manifest the new car, but an emptiness within will let you know that the new car is not going to give you the happiness you so desperately seek or thought you wanted. Something is missing. This is your divine aspect of you kindly letting you know there is something better out there for you, and deep down you know it.

Many cultures all over the world today have been practicing mindfulness for centuries. They understand being at one with yourself will show you the way.

Manifestation truly has many aspects to it. From my experience, when we become mindful and aware, exercising meditative practices, we connect to the source of our existence and our intentions begin to change, guided by the loving hand of Source.

Every day, time should be dedicated to sitting in silence with your eyes closed, doing nothing other than listening to yourself—no effort required. Many believe that meditation means sitting cross-legged and chanting OM, but that is one method. Meditation can be any activity that brings you joy, whether cooking, gardening, sailing, dancing, singing, or going for a walk.

Mindfulness develops your awareness; gives the human body a "tune-up"; allows you to calibrate your body, set your frequency, and adjust the dial to the awareness of what you seek. Developing awareness in your life will help clear out any negative and toxic thoughts you may be having.

As we are aware, thoughts are things; therefore, we need to ensure we can get to the core of the negative thoughts so they can be transmuted into positive affirmations.

Once or twice a day, time must be spent in practicing any form of meditation, to clear any negative thought patterns. The practice utilising mantra or mindfulness meditation has proven effective to use in order to control negative thoughts or even eliminating them completely.

Your mind strongly holds and believes what you pay attention to.

You are free to choose what you pay attention to.

Everything is a choice. You are responsible for focusing on the things you want to focus on. This is what we call power of mind.

"You are in control of your mind and thoughts."

Avoid negativity by focusing on a specific nonemotional object for a few minutes in the morning and in the evening. Let the brain focus on you. and ignore the thoughts. The feelings and sensations you experience during that time are priceless. Being mindful and empty of mind chatter of the day's activities is crucial. It is the first step and skill to master in this journey.

Another method we talked about is mantra meditation. Repeat a positive statement to induce positivity and combat negativity, especially when tired, frustrated, phobic, or worried and in distress.

Example Two outlines better responses to view your situation.

"I will succeed in everything I set my mind too."

"I am doing my best."

"This too shall pass."

Hopelessness and despair are very destructive and detrimental to one's health and mind power. Accept the importance by flowing and not resisting the process. Everything in existence flows. You will find that if you are not flowing, you are putting pressure on the universal flow of life, and that can only mean one thing; you cannot go anywhere, and honestly you will not be going anywhere. If you are persistent in resisting life, you will find that whatever cycle you are in will keep repeating itself until you learn to let go and allow that cycle to flow and move on. If you don't do this, that outcome can be very damaging. Just look at a dam that has too much water. The water has no natural flow but will build up until it spills over. Imagine what this resistance does to the human body. Disease—does this sound familiar?—denotes a body not at ease (dis-ease) with itself. I need say no more. I am sure you understand what I am getting at here.

"Flow with life and you will prosper."

Keep on taking action, growing, improving, learning, and understanding. Recognise your negative mind, and fill it with positive power. Keep in mind that negative thinking is natural, not 100 per cent avoidable, but manageable. Just keep on Flowing. Imagine a sailing ship sailing against the wind, going against the flow. Would it not be destructive to go against the natural flow or swim against the current?

You need to focus on having a clear idea about what to expect next from the future, an upcoming day or task. Dwell on an outcome while possessing a positive thought process, a healthy mindset, and optimism gleaned from good experiences. Align with the present moment. Only then can you achieve what you want. After all, everything does exist in the Now, and you need clarity of mind to be able to draw from the infinite Universe and claim at Will your desired outcome.

Finding clarity means having a clear understanding of what you want to achieve over time and how to move forward. It is about taking necessary steps when needed.

Today, there are many modern methods. Making SMART goals is one approach to take when it comes to preparing goals for your life, whether short- or long-term. Prepare goals daily, and review daily. Note that they must be:

Short
Measurable
Achievable
Realistic
Time based

An example of a SMART goal:

"This week I will meditate daily for twenty minutes before sleep to overcome negative thoughts and reduce their intensity."

Now closely take note how it is *specific* and short (meditate for a week), *measurable* (daily note taking to check if done properly), *achievable* (before sleep is the best time for it because it's calm, silent, and free of distraction), *realistic* (within capacity and easy to do by lying on bed with eyes closed and lights off with comfort level) and *time* based (twenty minutes per day).

Clearing off the mind has another method that directly attacks negative thoughts. This is done by creating a totally opposite *(positive)* thought by focusing on the positive and benefits of the situation.

We find it hard to have a positive outlook on life, as our mind is accustomed to having a sceptical approach to things, which usually includes the "what ifs" and "what happens" if you fail.

"Negative automatic thoughts are
something you can get rid of."

Remember the quote above wherever and whenever your pessimistic thoughts get the best of you and influence your state of mind as well as your actions.

What you focus on expands. Everything is within your choice. When you choose to give in to your negative thoughts, the outcome will be negative. However, when you focus your mind and energy on positive thoughts and make this a habit, you are able to see a significant transformation in everything you do. Over time you will naturally become that which you seek, and looking at positive outcomes will come with little effort and form a part of your existence, for you are one with it.

Motivation can have barriers if you allow it, and these may include confusion, unrealistic goals, loss of the sense of reward, poor strategy to do routine practice, and irrational thoughts and goals. It is common to experience all of these barriers. If you were not taught in infant years that you are in control of your reality, you will most likely have experienced all of the barriers outlined above.

Never give up ... Flow ... This too shall pass.

You must keep your motivation going and have the feeling of urgency to pursue what you want, as there is no such thing as the right time. Every second counts, and either you do it now or you don't. Remember that all we truly ever have is the present moment, Now.

I find that being mindful and aware of the present situation that you find yourself in gives you the ability to harness the attention required to maintain focus and keep the motivation flowing.

Here are a few examples that may assist in making a clear and concise plan of action. These examples are designed to take you a step forward towards your dreams, goals, and ambitions. As noted earlier if you are serious about creating a change in your life and you have the Will and Motivation, then take action!

Here's an Example of Action Steps that may be used:
- Keep your daily routine busy; use your attention for something valuable.

- Keep your mind filled with positive thoughts. This will influence your outlook on things and how you execute your day-to-day tasks.

- Practice an active lifestyle. Physical activities have a direct influence on both your mental and physical well-being.

- Keep your spirits high, and search for things that will help you stay motivated.
- Flow with Life.
- Always fill your thoughts with healthy, safe, and positive mantras/statements that you can relate with and will help you visualise your fruitful outcomes and polish the art of Manifestation for your self-designed destiny.

Maintain self-awareness. Become aware of everything in your environment, being mindful of all that is around you. For only you can control what you allow in and out of your environment. Observe everything. You are responsible for manifesting your dreams. Help yourself in making your dreams come true. Give credit to yourself for your positive mindset as well as coming this far.

Become that which you seek!

THREE

Visualisation

Imagination is everything. It is the previews of
life's coming attractions.
-Einstein-

If you can see it in your mind's eye, you can
create it."
Oh, so very True. Attracting that which you seek
success and prosperity whatever it may be.
Visualising creatively.
Your Desires must be created from within before
we see it in our reality. Everything in our
existence is a reflection from within. We live in a
reality of mirrors. Everything in our existence,
our current environment, had its origins in our
mind's eye.

"Inflect; then Self-Reflect."

The words in this book are igniting a memory within you—a remembering that you can harness your power and create at Will the life you want to live. So I remind you that you control the images and scenes you play out in your mind over and over.

We live in a world where energies draw other like energies to each other. Therefore, where you place your intended focus visually will create a magnetic charge drawing others like this. However, it must be followed through and imprinted into the subconscious. This can only be created through the action of repeating visually the scenario you want to manifest. If you visualise your intentions just once or twice, it will not have the needed amount of concentration, just as dunking a tea bag into a cup of hot water will not impart strength to the tea. Leave the bag in for some time, and the water will change colour, and the flavour and the full essence will start to develop. This metaphorically is the same for visualisation: you need to repeat the same image over and over again to create a level of concentration to create the essence of what you are intending.

Visualising your intentions works—and why would it not work? We visualise everything in existence before we create it physically. Architects visualise their design in their mind's eye before it is drafted and then physically built. It is the same for a chef, for an author, for an athlete, for everyone.

If it motivates you, you will carry out the necessary steps to create and manifest it into your reality. As you can see from the simple examples outlined above, we visualise everything. However, when it comes to bigger intentions, it goes back to the old adage we discussed at the beginning of the book: *You have to work hard to be successful.* There it goes again: life must be hard to have good things. Life is not designed to be hard. The prospect of working hard does not motivate anyone; it does the exact opposite. Unless what you are working on is something you enjoy, then we say to you that it is most likely that you are not on the right path. You have the tools embedded within to help you navigate your life.

There are tools you have not used, and some go through their entire existence never using them. Visualisation is one of these tools. If you visualise an intention and it feels right, allow your intentions to play out over and over in your mind's eye, and your heart will show you the way. There are so many who say, "But this is not what I had imagined for myself." You visualised yourself doing something completely different and took the option that was hard, thinking it was the only path to being successful. Maybe that is the case for some, but it is not lasting. Sometimes at most it is fear of stepping into the unknown that prevents someone from taking this step. It is something to work on.

> *"Always do what feels right for you*
> *—follow your heart."*

If you truly follow your heart, you can be assured you will be happy. If for some reason you are not, you did not truly follow your heart.

Visualising your intentions only requires five minutes a day, where you close your eyes and play the scene out in your mind's eye like a movie playing out. Visualise yourself winning your race, passing a test, opening your business, living in your forever home, always living in the final outcome. Alternatively, you can create a vision board, and you pin everything that you would like to be or achieve on this board and focus on that for five minutes daily.

Today, visualisation is utilised many fields from medical and scientific fields to aerospace. NASA has adopted the term *visual engineering*. Tests have also been carried out on individuals who were being assessed entirely by visualising an activity. During this process they found that those individuals who visualised the activity they had activated the exact same parts of the brain as someone would if they were physically carrying out the activity.

It is best to use visualisation daily for the achievement of your life dreams, goals, and everything you desire. As you learned previously on how to make SMART goals, you need to complement the daily goals with a detailed visualisation process.

The process of visualisation involves visualising the most effective way you would want to pursue your goal, as well as the feeling you have when you have finally achieved it.

The routine, anything that we do as a habit, is reinforced by a stimulus and reward. Positivity holds success; it raises our vibrations and brings us all closer to our dreams.

"What are you thinking?
Or are your thoughts on autopilot?

Changing your mindset does require the Desire and Will to carry out the necessary tasks. For some this will be easier to achieve, and for others it will take longer. It all depends on an individual's perception and motivation to keep doing a task daily for some time. You need to have the "Will" to keep carrying on. The length of time is individual, for everyone has different perspectives, levels of motivation, and levels of willingness. This is what makes us all Unique. No two people are the same.

Remember, we are talking about repeating the strategy countless times in our minds to reach that level of perfection. Practice makes perfect. At times it is the hardest of lessons that push us in the right direction. Like diamonds formed from high temperatures and intense pressure, we are the same.

What are some of the goals we want to achieve in our daily lives?

A job promotion, quitting smoking, starting a new business, finances for study—big or small, goals are goals and are the starting point for success.

The power of visualisation acts as a compass and can give you a better sense of direction to navigate your goals. The one thing you need is a lot of determination and trusting yourself in the process.

> A very famous and well-known quote
> says, "Seeing Is Believing."

Over two thousand years ago Aristotle also communicated this process, and it is still clear and applicable: if you first have an objective and then work for necessary methods to act, no one can stop you from your achievements.
The process of visualisation is important. It plays a huge rule in the manifestation of your goals as you have this mental image that you can achieve what you want.

Nothing is impossible when you believe. It gives you a sense of motivation that you are capable of doing even the unimaginable.

To manifest means to motivate yourself. Intrinsic motivation is something that has to do with "you". This looks complicated, but actually it is not. It only seems to be difficult because you have been thinking about trying something abstract and new.

Try visualising your goals by sitting in a quiet place for several minutes and closing your eyes. Focus on what you want and how you will achieve it. Don't let anything distract you in the process. When you are done, you will feel fresh and motivated in taking charge of what you desire.

Visualising your goals leads to the results that you want. Motivation stirs up the definite feeling of urgency, and the feeling of urgency is what makes you work towards creating your goals, turning them into reality.

As the saying goes,

> "The beginning of love is at the end of resistance."
> -Danielle Light

The very moment when you start to love yourself and defend yourself from negativity, all other things start to shift in your favour as well.

FOUR

Power of Affirmations

Repetition is the mother of all skill.
-Tony Robbins-

We all are designed to create our reality consciously. Constantly creating, evolving and expanding. Every word we utter, speak, scream, or think sends a ripple throughout all existence, just like a stone being thrown into the lake and forming ripples.

Nothing that we do is ever lost but returned to us because of our intention. What we draw to ourselves is a result of what we think about; it can be no other way.

It Is the Law of Attraction.

According to neuroscience and quantum physics, "Your mind is an energy field and responds to focus. Where you focus your attention creates brain connections. Quantum physics tells us that each of us generates energetic frequencies or vibrations. We project energy in our emotions and thoughts that are the source of what and whom we attract, as well as the basis of our sense of well-being."[4] We attract like situations to us on a continuous basis.

What Is the Law of Attraction?

The law of attraction is the ability to attract everything in our life that we focus on. It is all about manifestation, attention, and mental creation.

Why are the symptoms of anxiety in some people very apparent as compared to others? This is because they usually focus on the negative aspects of life and stress on it.

---

[4] Excerpted from David Krueger MD, *Outsmart Your Brain: An Instruction Manual: How Neuroscience and Quantum Physics Can Help You Change Your Life*, MentorPath Publications, www.NewBrainStory.com

They do not know how to let go of their problems and move on.

Positive visualisation of your goals is something you feel good about. The goodness and the happiness spread by visualisation is the subconscious attraction of achievement.

What creates achievement?

Have you ever thought about it?

Our achievements in life can be influenced by several elements in our life. This may include people we have around us as well as the kind of energy that surrounds us. The resources and circumstances we surround ourselves with do play a part in the achievement of our goals.

The law of attraction is the same for all human beings regardless of ethnicity, age, profession, religion, beliefs, nationality, and education. All human minds are subject to this law that rules our lives and eventually makes our thoughts into things we can touch.

Try this simple exercise.

Focus on a negative aspect and on a positive aspect of your life for one minute each. Start by thinking about the negative experiences followed by your positive experiences. Which aspect of your life is more prone to linger in your mind?

The state of your mind and your outlook in life determines the achievement of your goals. Always be aware of your negative thoughts taking control of you. If you constantly have a pessimistic view on everything, it will be projected in your actions and influence the outcome of your goals. Therefore, try your best to see the best in every possible situation. Even though sometimes things can get difficult, remember, there is always light at the end of the tunnel.

Many famous people throughout all time knew about and utilised this power, including some of the greatest personalities in history. The influencing names are Aristotle, Plato, Shakespeare, Blake, Emerson, Newton, Buddha, Jesus, Nikola Tesla, Henry Ford, Galileo, Einstein, James Allen, Beethoven, and Carl Jung. Today we have Tony Robbins, Eckhart Tolle, Matias De Stefano, Deepak Chopra, Rhonda Byrne, Neale Donald Walsch, and countless more; the list goes on.

It does not matter what your interests are—the arts, the sciences, or philosophy.

The law of attraction can take you far and may help you in various aspects which include the following:

- Healthy love life and relationships

- Better social interaction and communication skills

- Money and wealth

- Mental and physical improvement

- Healthy life and self confidence

- Reducing anxiety and self-doubt, guilt, or shame

- Weight loss, fitness, and mindfulness

- Success and abundance

"You Are What You Think You Are."

The more we are in tune with our inner self, the more familiar we are with what we are truly capable of. Therefore, the way you perceive yourself and your worth is important. The more you see yourself in a positive light, the more you attain. In contrast, the more you think you are not good enough and not worthy of success, the more you lose.

Whatever you desire to achieve is most likely present in your head as a mental image and is preparing to manifest by the operation of the law of attraction.

The Power of Affirmation is vital to creation. We need to embed our intentions into our subconscious mind and replace old belief systems, which may be limiting and negative, with a new belief system, one that is limitless and positive. The only way we do change limiting beliefs is to utilise uplifting affirmations and repeating these goals on a daily basis using the methods discussed in this book until they are formed in your reality.

Attention can only go where energy flows, and that is where you place your attention.

Affirmations have the power to encourage people to behave in a certain way. If anything, affirmations are uplifting and encouraging, truly helping you achieve your goals in life, giving power to change the negative thoughts and replacing them with positive thinking patterns.

The power of Affirmations reaffirms positivity back into your life and helps to increase your self-confidence.

FIVE

Taking Action

You are what you do, not what you say you do.
-Carl Jung-

The stage is set, all the details of your life are unfolded in front of you, and your affirmations are embedded into your subconscious. You now know that you are in control. You are limitless, abundant, successful, and powerful, able to achieve anything you set your intentions to.

The Universe is responding to your song.

You are the composer of the energy that flows through you and in you. Everything is taking place and now it is time to act. The leading star is you.

It is time. The fire burns within, and you hear a soft voice telling you to go for it. Do you trust this innate calling and go for your dreams, or do you ignore it?

When you hear the calling to Act, if it feels right to you—go for it. The adrenalin, the nerves, the excitement—the time has come to *act*. Do not ignore it.

What does this all mean - taking Action?

Taking action requires one to perform a deed, to execute something where it applies to the results as well. An action is short-term and continues to develop in a series of many small acts that result in a meaningful outcome.

Executing your plans and dreams is the most important aspect of your manifestation journey. Fear is experienced while you try to do meaningful tasks, but do not worry, as it is as natural as your dreams.

Fear kills your dreams more than anything else will. It is a common reason why people fail to act or achieve something simply because it is learned.

You are uncertain about the factors that might arise while taking action.

Consider this: fear is the biggest challenge of your journey of manifestation. It has been regarded as the "greatest enemy of humankind".

Successful renowned personalities including Winston Churchill and Franklin D. Roosevelt have written quotes on fear that depict their grasp on this hindrance towards achieving your dreams.

Some examples of their famous quotes:

"I'm waiting for someone or something to help or happen."
"You are incapable of believing in your own
power, confidence and self-esteem."
"I don't have time to start."

It is about self-belief and priorities. If your goal is important, you will always make time for it. It shows the significance of drive, energy, and motivation to charge forward and achieve your goals.

"There are already people doing it better than me."

You quit before you even start.

"I don't know where to begin."

These are all excuses which show you are letting fear get the best of you instead of searching for the answer on how to start.

"I don't think I'm making any progress."

No story of success is without perseverance and action.

Remember, fear is not real. It is all made up in your head and will get the best of you if you focus your energy on it.

How did you dare to dream if fear is rational?

Imagine what it would it be like if you were not afraid of manifesting your dreams. Truth is, you can unlearn the fear and embrace courage by the different steps we have been explaining since the start of this book.

Remember how you learned to read, to walk, and to talk? How did you overcome the fear in doing so? How did you have the courage to learn new things? Just like this: the bad habits including fear can be unlearned and be replaced with courage.
Ignoring the ups and downs of life is impossible, and dealing with fear is in your control. The lesson to be learnt here is to overcome fear.

This fear includes fear that has been rooted since childhood when your loved ones said, "Don't do that," and "You cannot do this."

The challenges in life strengthen the courage you have within you. The conditioning you have experienced since a child has two types of fear rooted inside of you; fear of failure and fear of rejection. This is your real enemy. Realise, recognise, and accept it, and construct your courage. This is your central action.

Ask these questions to resolve your deepest fears:

What would I have to do to eliminate fear?

How would I set myself free of my fears?

What is feeding this fear?

The emotion of fear is linked with unhappiness and stress, and to eliminate fear you need to have unshakable self-confidence and the courage to open the door of possibilities. It is relatable that "The only thing we have to fear is fear itself."

As Clement Stone stated beautifully, "Thinking Will Not Overcome Fear, But Action Will." This is fact: fear is an abstract concept that has gained our attention to make its place and create doubt on the road to success. Know that how you must eliminate fears out of your mind, daily and moment by moment, is by action.

Usually, it is the results you are afraid of, not the action or the plan. You have learned the unpleasant consequences that follow when things go wrong.

From today, each time you feel fearful, turn the consequence into a pleasant imagination. Use visualisation as a tool to foresee a successful outcome resulting of fear. What's more important is to focus more on the journey, than the results.

Just do it—we often read and hear it from others.

What is its true essence?

If you stand in front of an animal you don't like and you are asked to take them in hand, you probably fear the sense of touch and experiences that you would perceive and hence do not act to finish the task.

How about if you suddenly try something you have never imagined doing?

You don't know how to swim and have a phobia towards it, but after a few seconds of panic and shock, you start seeing that it's all right and it is not harmful. Another approach that promotes action is the initiative without overthinking and deciding to do something at a specific place, day, and time. Just do it!

Once you have successfully done something, letting go of your fears and visualising success, your dedication pays off.

This will inevitably boost your confidence. You have the skills to plan and the ability to act and handle challenges, improving areas where you lack. All of this is much more worthwhile than anything else. Meet new people, seek social and moral support, and enjoy the whole process.

Don't wait. After one step is completed, put forth the next step, and take action. Be physically recharged and mentally healthy, take short breaks at short intervals, and set aside the mental obsessions regarding perfection, comparisons, fears, and what-ifs.

Take your time to act out, and take a pen to write down your experiences and any intense negative emotions, and erase the large segments of self-loathing. Disposing of this burden makes you feel great about yourself, aids the manifestation of outcomes, and facilitates the process in achieving it.

Fear is loaded with procrastination, laziness, and irrational thoughts. Take your own time and pace to manifest your own steps moving forward, and do not be too hard on yourself.

The key is in your hands, and now you are opening the door to own your dreams and biggest desires of your life.

Taking action is what truly matters. Think clearly, count the number of times when you think about goals, and compare that with the number of times when you take action. The thoughts and mere plans would obviously outnumber the times you take action.

Think of problem solving, and execute your thoughts or plans by taking action. Problems are part of life, and you will confront them on your journey to success often. Prepare in advance about how you approach and overcome them.

"Start small, and consistency is key."

Let's imagine whatever you want to be—for example, a skilful chef. It's impossible for you to create five-star dishes when you've just started out. You need some time to learn and practice. That's why it is important for you to set realistic goals and be consistent in achieving them. Practice simple recipes first with simple ingredients, and then carve your way up to more complex processes.

Let's assume that you have determined the steps of taking action for a plan or a goal. To be more effective, write down a goal and write down the plans for execution in five to seven simple steps.

Review your own plan from time to time, and tweak it according to your progress because there is no one so desperate to achieve your goals as you are.

Make sure your plans and goals turn into action effectively, for efficient progression needs to be done gradually and in a consistent manner. Ensure and carefully plan the sequence in which the plan will be implemented, step by step and with grace.

The orderly structure and points from which you need to take action are of utmost importance. Sequence matters when you are planning to execute a long-term goal or plan. Long-term plans always have some systematic steps and orderly management.

Develop an effective action plan to implement after your goals are sequenced. Make sure a timeline guides each step. The next phrase is to carry out the plan. Do not be overwhelmed by the long list of goals and steps for each goal.

Prioritise and pick one goal that demands urgency, which you can execute immediately. In this stage immediate goals are the focal point. Bring all steps of the goal together, and analyse them as an overall task. Note the potential challenges the specific goal might involve, and list management options for the probable challenges. It is also necessary to include contingency plans to anticipate challenges leading to barriers. A few common examples are low financial resources and lack of time and energy or attention and interest.

Look cautiously at the lists and items you have in your action plan, along with the management plan as a backup. Keep moving towards success using a wide variety of methods. A blend of different activities never lets you down.

Human imagination is endless; no doubt it focuses on bad more than good while we start taking action; for instance, will you face success or failure? Imagination rushes to answer.

What are the chances of you losing?

But now our main focus is centre of attention. If for some reason something would not work, what would be the reasons, and how would you improve the situation? How can you increase the chances to win and be a better version of who you are?

Plan again: add something more to save you, motivate you, and make yourself a better winner. The new things you have seen since you first took action also go into the plan when you sit back relax to evaluate it again and assess where you started and where you are presently.

Final step is defining goals, whether to change your job or seek higher studies.

Attitude is everything you need. Mark dates on a calendar. Collect information from administrative offices, and highlight program details such as courses, schedules, and fee structure. Ask for help where needed, and set a reward for the completion of goals like buying a new cycle to attend classes on time and not missing any.

Action is materialising your thoughts into actions because ambitions are always packed with challenges and struggle. Achieving such goals requires an action plan and strategy to have hands on your goals you want to achieve.

Be realistic, stick to facts in action in contrast to the plans, visualise rational outcomes, and visualise what you expect for you to transform your life.

Do not be too hard on yourself no matter how hard it may be during the execution of your action plan. Completion is also a new beginning.

SIX

Gratitude

Have an Attitude of Gratitude.

As we gaze into the mirror, our reflection staring back at us changes each day. We are always reminded how our experience in this incarnation, in this lifetime, is fleeting.

Be grateful for making it thus far. Our life journey is really what we make of it.

"With appreciation all things Expand and Grow."

Adopting an Attitude of Gratitude can really shift one's perception from thinking unhealthy thoughts to appreciation, with awareness of what is around you and a growing sense of compassion for those around you. We are all in it together. It is a tough journey if we don't know how to utilise the abilities we have within.

Gratitude increases happiness and helps us develop a more positive outlook in our lives. We cultivate a genuine appreciation for what we already have and are able to pause for a moment and reflect on something in our lives right now that we are grateful for.

Our lives are our lessons we must learn from, and we are given endless opportunities to expand and grow. Everything from the time we are born has influenced and shaped us to be the person we are today.

Even more, we are here to Master our Reality! Mastering your reality is something you naturally adopt; it cannot be forced. A person must want to change for true change to occur.

We can only draw to ourselves similar energies. We also repel energies that are not on the same wavelength. This is a fundamental principle of the law of attraction. I am not really teaching anything new, as we go through this energy processing every day of our lives.

Our perception is everything. In our lives we need to constantly adjust our dials so we keep resonating to a tune that brings us joy and happiness.

Mastering your reality is a choice. No one but you can take action and take control of your life. Nobody can control another. This is a divine violation.

"Your Power lies deep within you."

Being grateful and aware opens the doors for new and exciting opportunities.

Gratitude changes us and our brain. Having an "attitude of gratitude" improves our mental health. Look around you; those who are grateful for things in life are happier and less depressed. Gratitude for all that we have in life— as opposed to what we want or think we need—is true happiness. You can shift your mood entirely if you focus on what you are simply grateful for today. Saying thank you is one way, but another way is to focus on what you like about yourself that you are grateful for—even more, if you are in a relationship, what you are grateful for in the person next to you.

If we pause and look around us, we will notice and appreciate the things that we often take for granted; like having a place to live, a bed to sleep in at night, food, clean water, the company around us, and friends and family.

It is taking this time to reflect on how fortunate we are right now. Being grateful for all that we have in life is True Happiness.

Even more, you are a divine being having an earthly experience just like everyone else who resides on this planet. Everyone has a journey just like you. Be considerate of one another, and most of all, don't judge what you do not understand. Be grateful that we are all in it together to expand and evolve together consciously.

Everything is a choice; nothing is a mistake. It is therefore your choice whether to be grateful; it is also your choice if you choose to be ungrateful.

There are some simple things you can do to begin practicing gratitude:

- Appreciate everything, even the small things.
- Give at least one compliment daily, or share your appreciation of something.
- Sit down daily and think of five to ten things you are grateful for. Then picture them in your mind, and enjoy the feeling of gratitude in your body.
- Say thank you more often and with a smile.

Learn to see the light of all things—a shift in perception is all it takes.

We are inherently designed to manipulate the energy around us. When we choose to be grateful, we change the energy field around our physical bodies, by changing the frequency and vibration and elevating the energy that surrounds us to a frequency of positivity. Gratitude is another way we can exercise daily to manifest and create a reality that we desire. Thus, this shift in energy draws to us like energies.

With an Attitude of Gratitude, we give appreciation to all things in life and with this appreciation the universe will return the appreciation one hundredfold.

SEVEN

Quantum Connections

Our words have a ripple effect throughout the universe.

Deep in this universe,
A signal is sent rippling throughout the galaxy.
Particles are forming an interconnected web of
consciousness.
They mirror that which I verbalised, visualised,
and seeded.
Magnetically charged, my signal is returning to
me with a gift.

It all began with the Word—I AM.

The words we speak are very important. Even more, there is Power to the phrase I AM.

I and **Am**—the Essence and the Existence

Everything we verbalise about ourselves starts with I AM. Therefore, it is wise to say that the most powerful words in this existence are

I AM

Many don't realise that we have given a name to our physical bodies, but it doesn't label who we are. For example, we cannot ring work and say our body is not coming in today. We have given our physicality a name.

Who we are at a soul level starts with I.

If you are to truly master your reality, rather than saying Jo is abundant, you need to speak from a soul level, not from the body, and verbalise the following:

I am Abundant.
I am Healthy.
I am Happiness.
I am Beautiful.
I am Love.
I am Joy.
I am Peace.
I am Gratitude.
I am Strength.
I am more than enough.

As we verbalise our intentions and go through everything, as revealed in this book, all that we have outlined is showing or revealing to us that we are constantly changing or manipulating the energy field that encompasses our whole being.

Energy is our life force that flows through us and in all things. The source of our power is the key to creating anything that we desire.

By changing the energy field that surrounds our being, we send signals from our core out in all directions. The signal is released out into the universe. It is never lost but returned to us.

This energy field that surrounds us is magnetically charged and as we speak a word it has a frequency and a resonance to it.

For us to attract our desires, we must have a high, uplifting, positive energy. If we are vibrating a low frequency, we will continue to attract low and negative things. At times when we find that everything is not working and that things are not going the way we planned them to, we start to feel everything is going wrong. It's the energy we are putting out there that is returned to us through the magnetism we noted earlier.

As we all radiate energy constantly, we tend to feel other people's energy too. We have at times made the comment or heard the saying, "Trust the vibes you feel from other people." This energy is you sensing what level the other person is at, and it doesn't lie.

Sometimes when someone walks into a room full of happy people and this person is negative, everyone will automatically feel the sense of being uneasy and simply not want to be there. The air feels dense; there is a sense of tension. You are not making this up—what you have done is sense their energy.

Additionally, if you are with someone and you feel happy, relaxed, and comfortable, they are on a higher vibration and sending off a light energy.

Our energy field allows us to sense people standing right behind us even though we are not facing them. What has occurred is that they have simply stepped into our field of energy.

The energy that we are a part of and our connection to consciousness allow us to bring our intentions into reality—our reality.

"Just as ripples spread out when a single pebble is dropped into the water, the actions of individuals can have a far-reaching effect."
-Dalai Lama

It's all magnetic.

If we think of ourselves like magnets, we either draw other magnets to us or repel them away from us. The same principle applies to manifestation. If we are thinking something or verbalising our intentions, we are magnetically drawing like particles to us.
Every substance is made up of tiny atoms that contain electrons. The particles carry electric charges. The electric charge magnetises particles that are vibrating and resonating with our intentions to us and vice versa.

If you look at a greater scale—energy is present everywhere and extends to our planet Earth. There are Energy grids that exist all over the planet. These Energy grids are magnetic and electrically charged.
Also, if you carefully look, all ancient structures are sitting in one straight line across the globe with a superstructure built on top of an energy grid point on this line.
Furthermore, there are energy grids sitting above the earth's surface.
In ancient times these Energy grids served a special purpose and were an avenue of communication back then. Today we are utilising the grids that sit above our earth for our telecommunications and how we communicate to each other.

As we move towards a technological era, as humans we play a big part in this shift and are truly a great aspect of this shift.

We are born into this world on Earth to be manipulators of this energy. We create every single thing in our environment constantly. When we awaken to our reality, how it truly is—which is limitless, abundant, and joyful—we can expand our potential significantly.

"The Power lies deep within."

At a young age we are told we have to go to school, and we have to work hard to get somewhere in life. We don't even give humans time to form their own beliefs or to be themselves before we start categorising them into groups, classes, and categories. It is all a form of control, but truth be told, no one can be controlled.

No one can categorise you into any category, as it limits a person and makes them think they must behave in a certain way prescribed by someone who came up with a theory from a limited perspective and mindset.

The reality in which we live is one that defies logic and reasoning, and it comes from a finite mind and understanding that isn't open to the possibilities that exist all around us.

To change this, we have to tap into that universal supply of the All that is, to understand that we can't define our reality by someone's perspective. This is one aspect of why you have to form your own beliefs and become your own person.

Everything in our surroundings, from commercials on TV to our education, reflects belief systems that are not our own and are at times very limiting. They can really send the wrong signal that you are not in control of your life and that you are limited in what you can achieve.

You see it all around you when someone is living in conditions that are not healthy, surrounded with struggle and depression.

You have spent your whole lifetime mingling with other energies, forming patterns of thinking and doing that are not your own but became yours. Now you recognise these patterns as not your own and they no longer serve you. You decide to clear or change them.

You then awaken to your true power that lies within and you are no longer roaming around on autopilot. You become limitless and capable of so much more. In fact, you are the only one who can control your life, as you are the one who is also accountable for it.

If you can readjust your mindset and rewire your brain, you are capable of great things, and there is no limit to what humans are capable of.

You are a master manipulator of energy, with infinite possibilities at your disposal. Your physicality is made up of the same subatomic particles that exist in stars that have existed from the beginning of time.

Our physical bodies are made up of atomic particles. We have trillions of atoms in one cell, and in our body, we have trillions of cells that are constantly replenishing themselves.

Live the life you choose and not the one that has been forced upon or you feel you must live.

Live your dreams. Transmute your environment to one that is singing your song, resonating to your tune.

Your life is a masterpiece in the making, and with a splash of positivity, uplifting thoughts, a shift in perspective, practicing mindfulness, and cultivating gratitude, you create a life that is worth living.

You are worthy of great things in life, and there is more than enough for everyone.

~

Afterword

Upon reflection, this book has come from experiences I had early in my childhood and has grown stronger throughout my entire life. I always had a great sense of Knowing and understanding of life that many people do not. I guess they call this psychic ability, I like to see it as having a greater self-awareness, which allows me to instinctively know things many do not and to connect to my higher self. I remember having precognitive dreams of things before they occurred. This was and continues to be a normal part of my life and I have learned to accept this as who I am.

I am here to teach and help humanity grow collectively into a heightened state of consciousness, which is how it's been done for thousands and thousands of years. You see, we all are always growing and expanding, and in addition to this, we are here to evolve along with our planet. Our earth is conscious and alive.

This book is one of many to come. This is an introduction to consciousness and our current reality received through my connection to the divine with a message to all that we are Creators and creative beings, with the power within all of us to be in charge of our lives and to create it any way we see fit.

All humans on this earth are creators of their own lives, and it's important to highlight that. When we say you are the creator of your life, we literally are stating just that.

Being given this gift, I have written this book with the intention that it will trigger a remembering from within – your innate, so that you too will remember how truly marvellous you all are.

All the messages I receive come through to me as thoughts in my mind's eye, or when I am writing, I will write and at times poetically, knowing that I never have written this way before.
I have incorporated a few messages received from the divine. These poetic messages are messages guided by the loving hand of Source.

Messages from the Divine

I Am the Light!

I am the light,
the peace that lies within,
The love that exists everywhere.
I Am the Eternal Truth,
Source of All Existence.
You all are experiencing through me.
When you seek answers to all existence
and pray for answers to Life,
My messages flow to you,
yet you turn away from them.
Is it not the light you seek? The answers?
My messages come from places and people you least expect.
I don't need a league of followers,
for I am not the Ego
For **I Am**
Your Spirit that is buried within you,
Waiting for you to Acknowledge me
and
Awaken from Within.

Life Is Not All It Seems!

Amusing, is it not?
—that the light of all truths
Is all around you
And embedded within you.
Yet you still question
Your reality
As if it is a mystery!
Dear one,
There are no mysteries
In this plane of existence
You call Earth.
You are the answer
To all your questions,
To life.
Stop Looking Outwards
And Look inwards,
For in this silence you
Are one
With all that is:
Source Energy.

Think Twice

If You truly
Understand
The Power of
The words you Speak,
You will think twice
Before Speaking.

For Words are WE.

You Become what
You Think
and
Speak About.

I'm Everywhere

When you look at
another person,
you will find me there;
when you look in the
mirror I am there also.
I am the trees,
the birds in the sky.
I am the air you breathe.
I don't need to be found,
for I am in everything,
and I am Everywhere.

I Am, That I Am,

"The All" that is and ever will be.

About the Author

Eva Gajic is the CEO and Founder of the Innate Consciousness Network. She has a master's in architecture with a long career as an architect and director. Her passion is dedicated to helping others, and her Network is all about raising the collective awareness of the planet.

Eva has a great understanding of the metaphysical world in which we all live. Therefore, she provides teachings of consciousness through her connection with Source. Eva's abilities have been with her all her entire life, and her books are used to help people on their individual development whilst providing truths to who we all are.